"I would rather w[alk]
with a friend in the dark,
than alone in the light."

– Helen Keller

Contents

Poetry

From The Manse Window

Country Calendar

Illustrations by Jim Dewar and Mandy Dixon.

Morning Illumination

WHAT a world of miracles,
Of angel clouds and crescent moon
Still smiling in the morning sky,
As planes streak silver trails behind,
And restless rooks awake and cry!
What a gift, God's masterpiece
Of galaxies and mysteries,
Our wealth of nature's flowers and trees,
Of verdant valleys, mountains, hills,
Eternal, mighty, endless seas!
Morning – fresh absorbed I stood,
Awash with thoughts and morning light.
Filled with awe to hear birds sing,
I lifted up my heart with thanks
In gratitude for everything.

– Chrissy Greenslade.

Keep Smiling

Let's all make a little vow
Starting from today,
To find the very best in life
Whate'er may come our way.
Learning to be patient
If we feel inclined to snap,
Keeping cool and calm
Instead of whirling in a flap!
Showing off a cheerful smile
To banish that old frown,
Making sure we really won't
Let upsets get us down.
Kindliness spreads far and wide,
Brings comfort to each day;
The cost is small, the value great,
The thoughts in hearts will stay.

– *Elizabeth Gozney.*

Rescue Plants

At the garden centre,
You will nearly always find
Plants that no-one wanted,
Those are always left behind.

Bedraggled and abandoned,
Hidden out of sight,
No-one wants to buy them
Because they look a fright.

No verdant, thriving foliage
Or bursting flower head,
But you might spy a hint of green;
They're not completely dead.

There may be some kind person
Who would possibly deduce
They could be quite a bargain
Because they are reduced.

So rescue them and plant them
Where they really want to be –
Tended, loved and nurtured
In your conservatory.

– Maggie Primavesi.

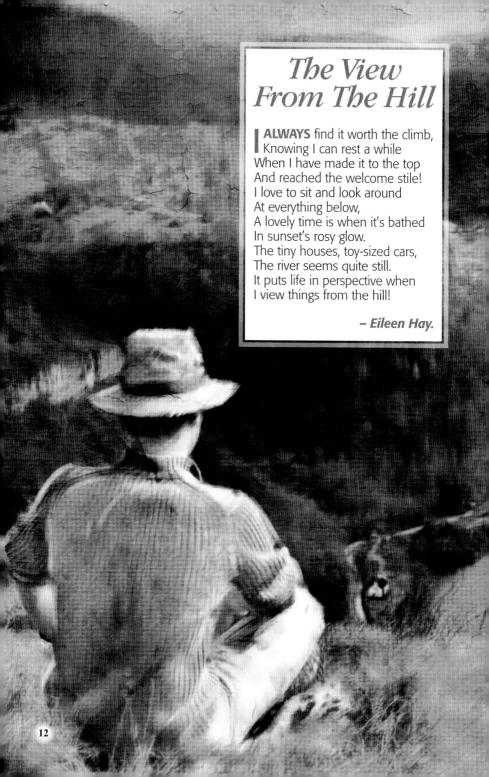

The View From The Hill

I ALWAYS find it worth the climb,
Knowing I can rest a while
When I have made it to the top
And reached the welcome stile!
I love to sit and look around
At everything below,
A lovely time is when it's bathed
In sunset's rosy glow.
The tiny houses, toy-sized cars,
The river seems quite still.
It puts life in perspective when
I view things from the hill!

– Eileen Hay.

The Soldiers Of Spring

IT is some time ago now, but I still recall the experience well. We had been having some hard winter weather, and although we were well into the new year, there was frost on the ground and a fair covering of snow on the gardens I was passing as I walked along the street.

All of a sudden I caught sight of something that uplifted my spirit. There, before my eyes in the garden I was passing, I saw a crocus that had managed to push its way through the frost and snow to raise its head bravely to the sky, a herald of the spring that was on the way.

That crocus struck me forcibly as being very brave, to be thrusting itself out despite the adverse conditions prevailing, in order to show itself as a harbinger of hope and joy to all who might care to look. It reminded me of this little poem:

In tunics, purple, gold and white
They lift their faces to the light
Of each new morning – unafraid.
Like tiny soldiers on parade.
And deep within its fragile heart
Each has a message to impart
Of sunshine, hope and glad rebirth
To cheer the winter-weary earth,
Bright crocuses, what joy they bring,
These gallant harbingers of spring.

I find it interesting that there is a mention of the crocus in the Bible, where Isaiah 35:1-2 says, "The desert shall rejoice and blossom, like the crocus . . . and rejoice with joy and singing."

The manner in which crocuses present themselves bravely to the world in the face of difficult conditions can be taken as both an invitation and a challenge to us. For one thing, it invites us to take heart, in spite of present distressing circumstances, in the sure confidence that, because of our trust in Jesus, he will bring us through our present winter, whatever it may be, to a new spring.

For another, it challenges us to be crocus-minded Christians doing our best (with his help) to be a source of hope and joy to fellow-travellers on life's highway, especially if they are facing painful circumstances.

The manner in which the crocus pushes itself bravely into view, sometimes in the worst of weather, is a valiant and comforting proclamation that spring is once more on the way, and indeed ▶

By the Rev. Dr James Martin.

▶ just around the corner, however unpleasant prevailing weather conditions might be.

To all of us, as we journey through life, troubles and sorrows are sure to come in some measure. The crocus certainly has a message to give to us if we choose to pay heed – a reminder that, come what may, the risen Jesus will have a springtime in store for us. It is also a call to us to be crocus-minded towards others experiencing a wintry season.

* * * *

The world owes a great deal to the brave witness and endeavours of crocus-minded Christians of past days. St Paul, for one. We may think of how brave a decision he made, in response to God's call, to leave his gospel-spreading labours in Asia and cross the sea to Europe, and embark there on the task of preaching the Gospel (Acts 16:6-12).

By all human standards it must have appeared that Paul was taking on an enterprise that was surely doomed to failure, because of the immense difficulties in the way of making a success of it.

What did happen, however, was amazing. The gospel flame that Paul ignited in Europe spread and spread, until it ultimately reached all over the known world. How grateful so many millions of people are today for the crocus-minded courage Paul displayed then.

Christians are indeed challenged to be crocus-minded, not least in today's society with its increasing secularism. They are challenged to lift up their lives bravely in the face of adverse conditions and deliver their Gospel message of hope, love and joy.

The world in which we live was perhaps never more in need of crocus-minded Christians.

THE daffodil also has a springtime message for all who care to listen to it. Let me tell you of such a daffodil message presented to me unexpectedly, but memorably, long ago in my student days.

I was travelling daily by bus from my home in Motherwell to Glasgow University which entailed journeying through the East End of the city, past a large area of not very attractive tenement housing. On the street level of these houses each building had been furnished at its foot with a small piece of ground between it and the pavement. For the most part these patches of earth were left untended and boasted no more than a crop of weeds.

One morning I was brought wide awake when I noticed from my upper deck window seat that one ground floor tenant had utilised his patch by digging it over to accommodate a lovely little group of yellow daffodils. By doing so he had transformed it marvellously. Enriched as it was now by a crop of bright yellow daffodils, that formerly desolate piece of neglected ground was virtually shouting out "Welcome to spring!"

Like the crocus, the daffodil has inspired poetry, such as these lines by Winifred Holtby:

My neighbour on her window-sill,
Has set a nodding daffodil.
I laugh to see it blowing there,
Golden and tall and debonair.
The boys and girls who never saw
So green and gold a thing before
Here linger with enchanted feet
To watch spring flowering down our street.

Crocus-minded? Daffodil-minded? These flowers certainly present an invitation and a challenge to all who care to open their minds and hearts to them. ■

A Country Calendar For *Spring*

> "In the spring, I have counted 136 different kinds of weather inside of 24 hours."
>
> **– Mark Twain.**

> "It was one of those March days when the sun shines hot and the wind blows cold: when it is summer in the light, and winter in the shade."
>
> **– Charles Dickens.**

■ *Did you know that spring onions are also known as syboes, green onions, scallions, salad onions, green shallots and onion sticks?*

■ **There is a spring festival in Egypt called Sham el Nessim. The name can be translated as "sniffing the breeze", and every year families enjoy a traditional meal of salted fish, green onions and coloured eggs outside in the fresh spring air.**

■ To keep cut flowers fresh, place the freshly cut blooms in cold water, not hot, and leave in the fridge for up to six hours before arranging them. Recut the stems every two days and change the water daily for the very best results.

Sold all year round now, hot cross buns are called "hot" because the buns were traditionally eaten hot or toasted on Good Friday, with the cross on the top representing the Crucifixion.

■ According to folklore, hearing lark song in spring heralds good weather and fortune. The songbird has also been used by Shakespeare and Chaucer as a symbol of daybreak and new dawns.

Golden Reminder

EVERY time I see them
They gladden everything.
If days are grey and dreary
They remind us all it's spring.

No matter if it's raining,
Or wind bows down their heads,
They bring much-needed sunshine,
Glowing bright in flower-beds.

My visitors and postman
Are cheered up by the sight
Of golden, frilled-cap daffodils,
Lifting spirits with their light.

I gave some to a sick friend
To spread love, joy and cheer.
She smiled. "How lovely. Daffodils!
Now I know that spring is here!"

– Chrissy Greenslade.

Nature's Gifts

BUTTERFLIES and buddleias,
A humming fluffy bee,
Seashells with their secret sounds,
The moonlight on the sea.
Spider webs with frosted gems,
The starlit sky at night –
These are some of nature's gifts
That fill me with delight.

Dewdrops on a velvet rose,
The golden flush of dawn,
Rainbows spanning stormy clouds
And daisies on the lawn.
Marigolds and buttercups,
Spring blossoms on a tree –
Work of a creative hand
For those with eyes to see.

– *Kathleen Gillum.*

April's Bounty

SUN, scattered showers
And glossy spring flowers,
A quintessential April morning!
Each raindrop a jewel –
Bright, sparkling, cool –
As fresh as the bloom it's adorning.

A glorious spread
Of tulips, deep red,
And daffodils, yellow and white:
Glittering gems
On tall, elegant stems
Stand radiant in bursts of sunlight.

The season of spring
In full, joyous swing
Brings rainbows and sunshine and showers.
As April flits through,
So refreshing and new,
Spring is breathing its life into ours.

– Emma Canning.

A New Life!

MY winter-flowering cherry tree
Failed to bloom at all,
With no leaves in the summer,
And dead before the fall.
So I grew a lot of clematis
To last the whole year through,
All colours you can think of –
Red, yellow, pink and blue.
It's now a tree resplendent
That blooms the whole year long;
Spring, summer, autumn, winter,
Its branches fill with song.
"What a transformation!"
My neighbours say to me.
"A new tree called clematis,
Born from a cherry tree!"

– *Dawn Lawrence.*

Maypole Dancing

DANCING round the Maypole
In days of long ago,
Brightly coloured ribbons
Are woven to and fro.

The children dance so happily,
Their hearts are full of joy.
It's such a very special day
For every girl and boy.

It is the merry month of May,
Cold winter days are past,
And so it's time to celebrate
That sunshine's here at last.

And even in our modern days
This custom can be seen
As, here and there, the children dance
Upon a village green.

It really is a pretty sight,
So let us hope that they
Will keep on dancing and enjoy
This lovely month of May.

– Rosemary Bennett.

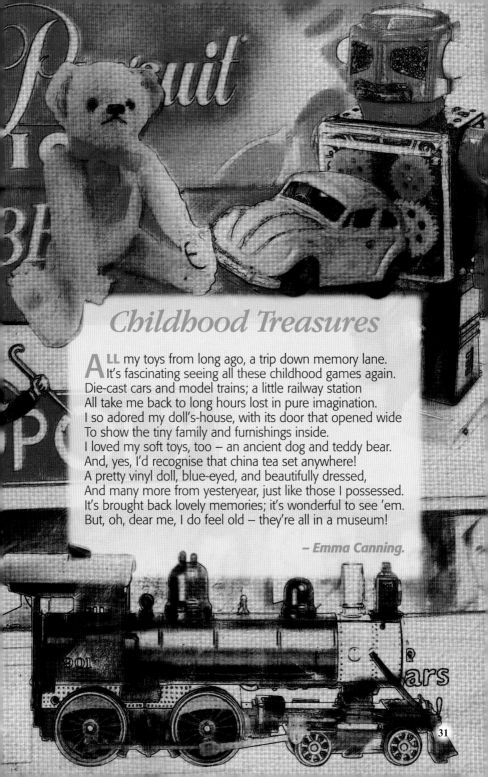

Childhood Treasures

ALL my toys from long ago, a trip down memory lane.
It's fascinating seeing all these childhood games again.
Die-cast cars and model trains; a little railway station
All take me back to long hours lost in pure imagination.
I so adored my doll's-house, with its door that opened wide
To show the tiny family and furnishings inside.
I loved my soft toys, too – an ancient dog and teddy bear.
And, yes, I'd recognise that china tea set anywhere!
A pretty vinyl doll, blue-eyed, and beautifully dressed,
And many more from yesteryear, just like those I possessed.
It's brought back lovely memories; it's wonderful to see 'em.
But, oh, dear me, I do feel old – they're all in a museum!

– Emma Canning.

Birdsong

THE air is full of birdsong,
A sweet, melodious sound.
It's nesting time, and eager birds
Are singing all around.

They sing to show the female birds
They'd make the perfect mate.
The finest singers have the edge,
The girls all think they're great.

They sing to mark their territory,
To let their rivals know
"This bit's already taken,
And I don't mean to go."

And though it's not intentional
There's something else they do,
They lift our spirits in the spring
And early summer, too.

Their cheerful chorus brings us joy;
It is our yearly treat
To hear the clear, enchanting sound
Of birdsong pure and sweet.

– Rosemary Bennett.

A Living Walking

DO you like walking? As the days grow longer, we can take advantage of the lighter nights, put aside the knitting, reading or television programmes that are the entertainment for those long winter evenings and have a stroll in the quiet of the day.

Until recently the people in the church did a lot of walking at this time of year, because processions – or just walks – are a traditional feature of the church event called Rogationtide (usually celebrated on or near April 25), although this custom has sadly fallen out of use lately.

I am sure that a good walk in the open air would unite all those taking part and ensure we realised just how many things we have to be thankful for.

The poet George Herbert described it as "a living walking" because it is not just an aimless wander, although there is nothing wrong with that if we just want to get out and about to look at God's creation. But this is a walk with a purpose.

It was very common at one stage for the people to use this walking to ask God's blessing on the crops, trees, plants and orchards nearby.

Another tradition soon developed from it, that of "beating the bounds", where a congregation would walk the parish boundaries to make sure that everyone knew where they were and what area belonged to that church. Of course, modern map-making means that this is no longer needed, but the tradition and this special day continue.

THE name of this special day comes from Jesus's promise to us that we are to "Ask and you will receive, so that your joy may be complete."

The problem is that a lot of people don't bother asking, and so they wonder why they haven't received!

This became an important promise in the lives of those from the rural communities of yesteryear, as they became aware of the fact that "All good gifts around us are sent from heaven above."

Their walk became a walk of praise and joy.

It is perhaps this sense of awe and wonder that is

Thinkstockphotos.

By Kathrine Davey, Mansfield Methodist preacher.

nowadays best reflected through the eyes of those younger members of our community – that is to say, those in whom the gift of new life is most apparent.

Signs of new life are everywhere, from the birth of the new-born lambs gambolling in the fields, to the new buds and flowers springing up where the earth had once seemed so bare and dead. Birds return from their wintering-grounds ready to build nests and produce their own young, and the time of winter hibernation gives way to a flurry of spring preparations.

Unlike the harvest festival, this is a "new life festival" celebrating what is about to spring out of the earth.

Around this time of year comes Easter Day, when new life is celebrated in all its fullness. Many people do not realise that this is not one isolated day, but is the start of the Easter season.

The usual phrase used at the start of many services taking place on Easter Day is "Christ is risen!" and the congregation answers "He is risen indeed!"

The 50 days of Eastertide are a time of great joy, when we have the chance to celebrate Christ's bodily resurrection.

There are numerous references to this throughout the Bible, and it is no surprise that all four gospels have an account of the Easter story, which is further emphasised by St Paul who made sure to tell us that our faith is in vain without the hope given to us in Christ's resurrection from the dead.

In fact, Easter has been described as "the pinnacle of our Christian faith".

EASTER is what we call a moveable feast, because the timing of it depends on the Jewish Passover and the phases of the moon. That is why some years Easter is early or late.

However, whatever the time of year, it is always a time to celebrate. And it always was, despite the uncertainty that those first disciples must have felt. They were still in shock, having to come to terms with an entirely new situation.

The Gospels record them hiding behind locked doors for fear of the authorities, or back fishing where they had been before Jesus had called them. They had returned to their previous way of life, convinced that the last three years had been a waste of time.

If only they knew! They were confused, and it was only later that this confusion would turn to joy.

It was while they were going about their daily business that they had one of their many meetings with the risen Lord. The same is often true in the modern world, as people do not expect to encounter him in such ordinary places.

The Feast of the Ascension (when the disciples see the risen Jesus leave this earth) falls within the Easter season. It is often forgotten that the 50-day season of Easter runs up to, and includes, the Feast of Pentecost. This is often

called the birthday of the church, because it was only then that those same confused disciples finally found the power to become the early church's first preachers and leaders.

Nothing is ever wasted in life, and that difficult three-year period proved to be a good training ground for their new lives as stalwarts of the church. ■

A Country Calendar For *Spring*

■ A great way to check if your garden is ready for spring planting is to pick up a handful of soil, form it into a ball and throw it on the ground. If it crumbles, your soil is ready; if it breaks in two or stays in its shape, your soil is not yet ready for planting.

"Spring makes its own statement, so loud and clear that the gardener seems to be only one of the instruments, not the composer."
– **Geoffrey B. Charlesworth.**

"The world's favorite season is the spring. All things seem possible in May."
– **Edwin Way Teale.**

■ Hawthorn, also known as Whitethorn and May blossom, like all thorn trees is supposed to be a sacred meeting place for fairies. May blossom was considered unlucky indoors because it was supposed to bring on illness and death.

■ In Roman mythology Flora was the goddess of flowers and the season of spring. Her festival, the Floralia, was held in April or early May and symbolised the renewal of the cycle of life, marked with dancing, drinking and flowers.

■ The first day of spring is also known as the Vernal Equinox. The sunrise and sunset are about 12 hours apart everywhere on Earth and the hours of daylight and night are almost equal.

■ A section of the border between California and Oregon is often called the "Easter Lily Capital of the World" as it produces 95% of the 11 million spring Easter Lily bulbs grown in the world each year!

Ode To A Slug

DEAR Slug,
You cannot eat my plants,
For I have toiled all day.
Their tiny buds will grow and flower
And in summer breezes sway.

The garden will be filled with joy,
A butterfly's delight.
So, instead of darkness's stealthy feast
Please try to sleep all night.

– Nicola Herington.

Weather Forecast

THE summer starts on Friday!
I saw it on TV.
The weather forecast said so,
That's how it's going to be.
Forget about the gusty wind
That blew us here and there,
And all the rain which soaked our feet
With puddles everywhere.

Let's have a bit of sunshine
To cheer us up a lot.
We'll have ice-cream and cooling drinks;
Who cares if it's too hot?
The summer starts on Friday.
Don't miss it when it's here,
But if the forecast should be wrong
Watch out for it next year!

– Iris Hesselden.

The Trickster

MY watering can was empty, so I filled it at my sink.
I thought, I'll give these plants a soak; be done in half a wink!
But though I tipped the can both ways, and shook it all about,
I found, despite my efforts, that no water would come out!

I swished the water up and down, and then from side to side,
But still no water came from it, however hard I tried!
At last I peered and poked inside, and there, inside the spout,
Was the reason why the water had trouble coming out.

A snail of large proportions had found the space just right,
And though I pushed and poked once more, it held on really tight!
I had to use both guile and wit to set the prisoner free;
If that ruse was a trick, I thought, the laugh was all on me!

– Dawn Lawrence.

My Wood Pigeons

THE birds that make me quite incensed
And want to rant and tear my hair,
Who ruin all my garden plants
Are that unruly, wicked pair
Of wood pigeons!

They dig up bulbs and new, young plants,
They gobble up each grain of seed.
The other birds don't stand a chance
Against the endless, awful greed
Of wood pigeons!

The welcome mat is always out
For every other garden bird,
For sparrows, blackbirds, robins, wrens –
Just anything but those absurd
Darned wood pigeons!

And yet, when sunset paints the sky,
The pergola washed in rosy light,
They snuggle up and bill and coo
And then I feel that I just might
Like wood pigeons!

– *Eileen Hay.*

The Garden Planner

THE garden centre beckons me
Whenever I drive past;
I always think I won't buy much.
That feeling doesn't last!

I can't resist the colours,
The scent of flowers in bloom,
With scant consideration
Of whether I'll have room.

I get a shock when paying
For my overloaded trolley,
And only when I'm driving home
Reflect upon my folly.

I still have pots galore to plant
From previous trips I've made.
I never quite get round to them,
They're on the bench arrayed.

I know just where to put them all,
They'll really look sublime,
But I'll have to weed the border first
And there's so little time.

I can't wait to see them growing
In my garden, in the sun,
But for now I'll water all my pots
And dream of when it's done!

– Eliza Barret.

Speaking Of Weather

I **REMEMBER** one September
When the summer just rolled on.
It remained quite hot and sunny
When it really should have gone.

We sat shirt-sleeved in the garden
Or went walking by the river;
We stayed out late each evening,
And no-one gave a shiver.

We all talked of milder winters,
And someone rumoured drought.
Nobody ever went indoors
While they could still be out.

Then came the day it went away,
In blew the autumn chill.
We had something new to talk about
And enjoyed it better still!

– *Norman Lindsey.*

Sweet Moments

I **LOVE** the art of tapestry –
Working thread and needle thru'
The many beautiful shades of wool
And creating patterns new.
A bouquet of flowers tied in a bow;
Starry night, with a harvest moon;
Strawberry heather and golden gorse;
Saffron poppies on a windswept dune.
Into the canvas, stitch by stitch,
The magic strands entwine.
Magenta, butterscotch, heavenly blues
And the greens of emerald and lime.
Chair covers, I've done quite a few
In the time set aside, just for me.
Contentment flows as I sit and sew,
Loving the art of tapestry.

– Dorothy McGregor.

Rex's Magic Mower

OUR neighbour Rex, who lives next door,
Has got this old machine,
All patched up where parts fell off,
With brown tape in between.
Our other neighbours' lawns are neat,
But not as Rex's is;
They stop and stare with rounded eyes,
"But why aren't ours like his?"

Other mowers are shiny new,
Much better, you'd have thought,
But Rex's mower outshines the rest,
It cuts the grass so short!
By the time he's finished mowing
With that taped-up old machine
His lawn looks quite magnificent,
Just like a bowling green!

Rex proudly says, "It does the job.
Like old things that still last.
It's a precision-made contraption,
A tribute to the past!"
If you think you might have seen it,
A few miles from your home,
I shouldn't be at all surprised.
It's probably "on loan"!

– Dawn Lawrence.

Here Comes The Summer

SUMMER brings great joy – long, warm evenings, the scent of the garden, blue skies and white fluffy clouds and lots of sunshine (hopefully). Neighbours see more of each other because they're outside in their gardens and people generally are more cheerful. Life seems to be filled with more possibilities, and for many of us there's the prospect of going away on holiday.

There's a song I learned a long time ago when I was in primary school which goes something like this: "Summer has come from the sunny land, summer is here again". I still sing it to myself sometimes as I'm driving along. We've waited a long time and now here it is! It always arrives, without fail.

There's a lot of joy in the New Testament even though we equate the ministry of Jesus ultimately with suffering on the cross – he was a Man of Sorrows, acquainted with grief. He and his disciples may have led a nomadic, often tough life, but there was joy in it, too, and camaraderie and fellowship as they worked together and relaxed at the end of the day talking over the day's events.

Imagine the joy of seeing people being set free from disease, possession or addiction, of seeing people being restored whole to their families! Joy must have been running amok through the Holy Land because people suddenly had hope. Somebody was doing something to change their lives and to make God seem real!

Jesus found great joy in Satan being challenged and thrown down. On one occasion he sent out 72 disciples to prepare the way ahead of him. When they returned they were excited at the things they'd been able to do in his name. Jesus was excited, too.

"I saw Satan fall like lightning from Heaven" (Luke 10:18).

Luke also tells us that Jesus was full of joy through the Holy Spirit. The defeat of evil brings joy and hope because it gives us a glimpse of how things are meant to be.

On the night before his death, Jesus speaks to his disciples.

Thinkstockphotos.

By the Rev. Susan Sarapuk.

▶ "I have told you this so that my joy may be in you and that my joy may be complete" (John 15:11). He knew that he was going to die and yet he speaks of joy.

CHRISTIANS should be summer people, for although we know that sin is serious, dark and bleak and destroys, Easter Sunday follows Good Friday and we have good news to give to people, not bad news. Jesus died but he is alive.

I think that was one of the attractive things about Jesus and about Christians in the early church. People sensed the life coming out of Jesus and his disciples and knew they wanted some of it. After Pentecost, the followers of Jesus were set free to proclaim the good news. They didn't care if they were imprisoned or forbidden to speak in his name. Stephen glowed as he was stoned to death; Paul and Silas were singing hymns in prison at midnight.

"In all our troubles my joy knows no bounds," Paul wrote in 2 Corinthians 7:4, and we know the difficulties he encountered in his Christian life.

So joy is something apart from our circumstances. True joy is a spiritual thing; it comes from God and can rise above the most terrible situations. It reminds us that life isn't about good things happening to make us happy. Joy is something else.

It was joy that created the universe. Consider the stars, all that exists in space, the things we are only just discovering about the existence of dark matter. What is the purpose of it all? I can imagine God creating for the sheer joy of it.

And God saw that it was good.

When we look at the heavens we're not meant to feel small and insignificant, or to worry about what's out there. We're meant to rejoice in a God who creates for the sheer joy of it and to know that we are the most special part of that creation.

This sort of joy can also be lost. Obviously we feel that loss when circumstances weigh us down, when we're ill or bereaved or bad things happen to us. What happens to our joy then? We become preoccupied with the bad situation we're in and can see no way out of it.

People say time heals. That can often sound harsh, even though it's generally true. We do come out the other side. If we are relying on good things happening to give us joy then we will be disappointed.

Paul wrote this to the Galatian church – "What has happened to all your joy?" (Galatians 4:15). They had drifted away from God; they had got caught up in division and argument and allowed their circumstances to weigh them down. They had forgotten the source of all good things.

God willing, we hope to live long lives full of experience and opportunity, but it is inevitable that somewhere along the way we will encounter grief,

sadness and difficulties. If we leave God out of the equation then our joy will be dependent on our circumstances and we will lose it because no-one can live a life without troubles.

But if we know we are walking this road with God, that everything has a purpose and no experience is ever wasted, then we can find that joy deep in the centre of our being where God has made us to live in communion with Him. After all, it can't be summer for ever. Winter will come again, but even in the cold and the rain with the dark nights, the bare trees and the bare garden, we know that summer will come again, too. That, ultimately, everything will end in summer. And it is in that anticipation that we find great joy! ■

A Country Calendar For Summer

■ In Paris, the Eiffel Tower can be just over six inches taller in the summer due to its 7,300 tonnes of iron expanding on hot summer days.

"What good is the warmth of summer, without the cold of winter to give it sweetness?"
– John Steinbeck.

"Summer afternoon, summer afternoon; to me those have always been the two most beautiful words in the English language."
– Henry James.

■ The quality of television programmes really is worse in the summer as, due to lower viewing figures, the TV schedules include more reruns, keeping new episodes of their most popular shows back until September when viewing figures rise again. The music and film industries, however, experience higher returns during the summer months than any other time of the year.

HD TV

Thinkstockphotos.

■ Red peppers are more mature than green, orange or yellow peppers. They contain almost 11 times more beta-carotene than green peppers, as well as one and a half times more vitamin C. The favourite colours of pepper, for taste, tend to be the sweet red and orange ones, followed by the mildly sweet yellow one, with the more bitter green one in last place.

The first day of summer is called the summer solstice, which is Latin for "sun stand still". In Finland the midsummer celebration is one of the biggest of the year with bonfires and festivals throughout the country.

■ "Summer is Icumen In" or "Summer Has Come In" is the oldest English round song yet discovered, and dates back to the 13th century.

Sunlit Shore: A Meditation

THE sunlight sparkles on the sea,
All nature wears a smile,
And we will leave today behind
For just a little while.

Soon we travel back in time
As years all slip away
And we exchange all troubled thoughts
For sunlit yesterday.

We take the path along the cliffs
Where gentle breezes blow.
We are refreshed in heart and mind
And feel an inner glow.

The path leads down towards the shore
And we walk hand in hand,
And there the children play and build
Their castles in the sand.

They search for rock pools, look for crabs,
Collecting many shells,
Whilst sunbeams dancing on the waves
Are weaving magic spells.

A little kiosk, painted green,
Supplying pots of tea,
Has fizzy drinks and ice-cream cones.
They're tempting you and me.

But as we saunter on our way
The tide comes creeping near,
And many happy memories
Are all created here.

And so we leave this sunlit shore,
Returning to this day,
But happy times, like children's rhymes,
Will never fade away.

– *Iris Hesselden.*

Pottering

I LOVE to have a potter,
And that's the simple truth.
In fact, I started pottering
Way back in my youth.
I pottered in the playground,
I pottered round the school,
I pottered in the bike shed
And by the swimming pool.
Now I potter in the greenhouse
And nip those side-shoots out.
I heap up the potatoes and
Wait for them to sprout.
I potter in the garage,
My tools laid in a group.
I water my geraniums
When I see them droop.
Every year, on holiday,
I potter all the time.
What better place to potter than
By rock pools, sand and brine?
So, now the summer time is here
And the weather's getting hotter,
If you'll please excuse me,
I'll just wander off and potter . . .

– Brian H. Gent.

June

ALTHOUGH it's known as "flaming June",
At times we say this far too soon,
For cool fresh winds may come our way
Before the warmth decides to stay.
But stay it will, so have no fear,
We'll feel June's heat again this year.
As sun shines down on yonder shore
We'll welcome flaming June once more.
With spirits lifted, we will smile –
Our wait for June has been worthwhile!

– Joan Zambelli.

Our Favourite Beach

A **SURFER** braves the silver waves
In churning, frothy seas,
Our cheeks now glowing; kites are blowing,
Tossing in the breeze.

Rooks proudly stalking, shrill gulls squawking,
Displaying in the sky,
Dogs madly racing, chewed balls chasing,
Wind-blown passers-by.

Islands gleaming, sunlight streaming
Its sunbeams on the sea,
Children are fishing, mothers dishing
Steaming cups of tea.

Loaded, home-going dads soon towing
Chairs, balls, bucket and spade.
As turning tides our presence hides,
Seabirds return and wade.

A rosy sunset helps us forget
Coolness in the air,
It's time to go, but we both know
That we've left our hearts there.

– Chrissy Greenslade.

Hot Summer Days

THE breeze blows the beech trees, the wind wafts the willows,
Clouds float on high like fluffy white pillows,
A clover-clad meadow's sweet scent in the air,
As cabbage white butterflies flit here and there.
The wave of the wheat stems in faraway places,
Calves, newly born, show their little fresh faces.
Thrushes in bushes and lambs on the lea,
And, way in the distance, there sparkles the sea,
With sand that seems endless and donkeys that jingle,
With holidaymakers who jostle and mingle.
Such are the magical mystical ways
That manifest only on hot summer days.

– Brian H. Gent.

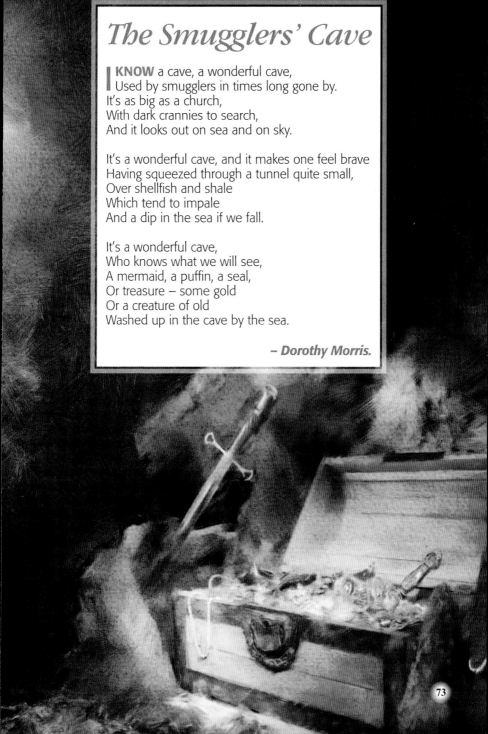

The Smugglers' Cave

I KNOW a cave, a wonderful cave,
Used by smugglers in times long gone by.
It's as big as a church,
With dark crannies to search,
And it looks out on sea and on sky.

It's a wonderful cave, and it makes one feel brave
Having squeezed through a tunnel quite small,
Over shellfish and shale
Which tend to impale
And a dip in the sea if we fall.

It's a wonderful cave,
Who knows what we will see,
A mermaid, a puffin, a seal,
Or treasure – some gold
Or a creature of old
Washed up in the cave by the sea.

– Dorothy Morris.

Healing Blue: A Meditation

DEEP blue the sky above the distant fells,
A gentle blue the shadows on the hill,
And as the evening travels down the valley
A grey-blue mist lies where the land is still.
Now, as the silence wraps itself around us,
Warm memories come softly creeping in.
So many times the healing blue of nature
Can soothe the spirit and the soul within.

We journey back to far-off childhood times,
To bluebell woods where we would run and play.
A blanket spread where we could share a picnic,
The simple pleasures of a bygone May.
A memory of walking by the river,
Blue sky and clouds were both reflected there,
Or pausing on the seashore in the evening
To watch the tide and simply stand and stare.

So often in the winter there is wonder
When snow lies deep and still upon the ground.
Blue shadows fill the crevices and hollows
And there is beauty still, it's all around.
So look for healing blue; it's all about you,
In lakes and rivers, pools and sparkling streams,
Forget-me-nots, in iris and in lupins,
And let that colour calm and fill your dreams.

– Iris Hesselden.

Following Holy Footsteps

RECENTLY Margaret and I fulfilled a lifelong ambition and embarked on a pilgrimage to the Holy Land. From Edinburgh we flew south to Heathrow and then on to Tel Aviv airport where we were met by our guide for the pilgrimage, Oliver. What a wonderful guide he was! Oliver's knowledge of the history of that land was extensive and at times breathtaking.

We were stationed in Jerusalem and later on in Tiberias in Galilee and at both venues we stayed in the accommodation the Church of Scotland owns. In both these places there is a church, too – St Andrew's Scots Memorial Church, Jerusalem and St Andrew's Church at Tiberias.

For several years the Church of Scotland has had property in the Holy Land. The Scots Memorial Church and Guest House in Jerusalem was completed in 1930 and the Scots Hotel in Tiberias was set up originally away back in 1894 as a Mission Hospital. A twenty-three-year-old surgeon from Airdrie set up the Mission Hospital to preach the gospel and to care for all in that land, irrelevant of race, creed, class or colour. Today the old hospital has

been transformed into a very comfortable hotel which hosts pilgrims from all over the world.

We saw so much in the course of our short pilgrimage, and it was wonderful to see so many of the places and sites that I have been talking and preaching about throughout the course of my ministry.

Early on we visited the Church of Pater Noster on the Mount of Olives. It was here that Jesus taught his disciples the Lord's Prayer and that immortal prayer is inscribed on the walls of the cloister of this church in over 60 different languages, including Gaelic and Doric.

Later on we climbed the Mount of Olives to a place called Dominus Flevit. It was on this spot that "Jesus wept" over the city of Jerusalem and interestingly the tower of the church now built on this site is in the shape of a teardrop.

Soon we were in the Garden of Gethsemane before making our way to the Via Dolorosa along which Jesus carried his cross. Margaret and I were privileged to read the Scripture passages relevant to each Station of the Cross along the weary way Jesus had taken.

Thinkstockphotos.

By the Rev. Ian W.F. Hamilton.

▶ Finally we reached the Church of the Holy Sepulchre, which is at the very heart of the Christian faith. It is this site which encompasses all that remains of the traditional rock of Calvary and the site of Jesus's tomb and to be there was moving, to say the least.

Later on in our pilgrimage we visited Bethlehem. The main feature of this world-famous town is the Church of the Nativity which is built over a cave where, according to strong tradition, Jesus was born. We celebrated communion in the Shepherd's Fields nearby before heading to Nazareth where Jesus worked in the carpenter's shop with Joseph his father.

Soon we were on the banks of the River Jordan, where we are told that John the Baptist baptised Jesus. All the ministers on the pilgrimage took the opportunity to fill a bottle with "Jordan" water. I used mine the following Sunday back home to baptise a little boy named Joshua!

A MONG the pilgrimage venues which followed were Cana, Nazareth and Capernaum. It was at Cana in Galilee that Jesus performed his first miracle by turning water into wine at a wedding feast and the Franciscan church we visited there is known as "The Church of the Wedding Feast".

When we reached Nazareth we went to see the Synagogue Church. This small Greek-Catholic church stands on the site of the synagogue in Jesus's day where he was taught and where he learned to read. Of course it was here also where Jesus is said to have read aloud the Scriptures and proclaimed their fulfilment.

The excavated archaeological site at Capernaum is one which is of major importance to Christian people, because Capernaum was adopted by Jesus as his "home town" after he was driven out of Nazareth. It was in this town that Jesus called Peter, Andrew, James, John and Matthew to follow him and also here the Gospels record Jesus as having performed several miracles. Jesus also worshipped and taught in the synagogue in what in his day was a very busy fishing port.

The two main features of Capernaum today are the partially reconstructed fourth-century synagogue which has been built on the foundations of the synagogue in which Jesus had preached. The second main feature at Capernaum is a late 20th-century church which has been erected over the site of a house which the Franciscans claim was owned by Jesus's disciple, Peter. Capernaum was a very special place.

Towards the end of our pilgrimage we visited the Sea of Galilee, even sailing across that famous sea! We stopped at a spot on the shores of the Sea of Galilee called Tabgha where Jesus multiplied the five loaves and two fish which a wee boy once brought to him to feed a vast crowd.

We went into two churches there; first of all the modern church known as "The Church of the Multiplication" with many beautiful fifth-century mosaics built into its floor, and secondly the "Church of Mensa Christi" (Table of Christ), a little chapel constructed on a rock at the water's edge. This is the spot by the lakeside where

Jesus, according to tradition, appeared to his disciples following his resurrection.

It was around this lakeside spot that I had the wonderful privilege of celebrating Holy Communion for our group of pilgrims. Words could never express the inward feeling of peace as I held the bread in my hands and lifted up the holy cup, to the sound of the waves lapping on the shore behind me.

The story of the loaves and fishes was a sacramental meal, too, because although it would only be a mere morsel each received from Jesus, the wonder of his presence turned every sacramental crumb into something which richly nourished their hearts and fed their souls.

This happens every time wherever Holy Communion is celebrated, but you can be sure that it certainly happened for our group of Scottish pilgrims, when we broke bread together and shared the cup of salvation "beside the Syrian Sea". ■

A Country Calendar For Summer

"A perfect summer day is when the sun is shining, the breeze is blowing, the birds are singing, and the lawn mower is broken."
– James Dent.

"The first week of August hangs at the very top of the summer, the top of the live-long year, like the highest seat of a Ferris wheel when it pauses in its turning." –
Natalie Babbitt.

■ The sound of chirping crickets has become synonymous with long, summer evenings, but did you know you can tell the temperature by them? The frequency of a cricket's chirps fluctuates with the temperature, so if you count a cricket's chirps for 15 seconds and add 37, you will have the approximate outdoor temperature in degrees Fahrenheit!

■ "Dog Days of Summer" refer to a period of heat and lethargy during the summer months. The phrase is in reference to the dog star, Sirius, which rises and sets with the sun between July and September. This synchronicity was thought by the Ancient Greeks to cause the extra heat.

The American ice lolly, or popsicle, was invented by accident by eleven-year-old Frank Epperson. He left his glass of powdered soda outside one cold night with its stirring stick in, and by morning it had frozen. Tasting it, he found it delicious and eventually patented the idea in 1923.

■ One of the most summer-loving flowers is Cosmos bipinnatus, which needs full, direct sunlight and a minimum of 24 degrees Celsius (75.2 degrees Fahrenheit) to germinate!

■ **The Ministry of Agriculture launched one of the best-known slogans ever just one month after the declaration of war in 1939 – "Dig For Victory". By 1943 over a million tons of vegetables were being grown in gardens and allotments.**

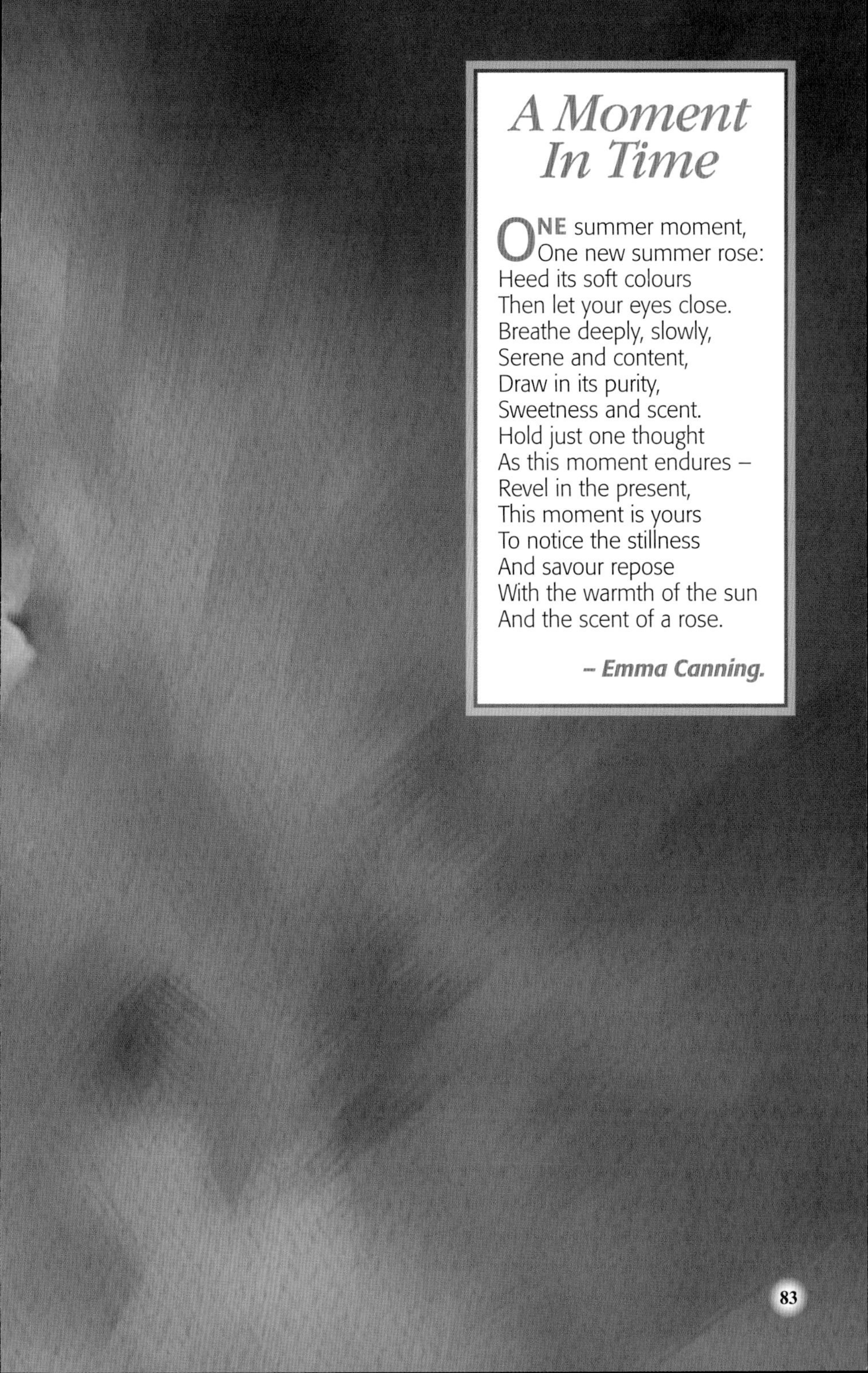

A Moment In Time

ONE summer moment,
One new summer rose:
Heed its soft colours
Then let your eyes close.
Breathe deeply, slowly,
Serene and content,
Draw in its purity,
Sweetness and scent.
Hold just one thought
As this moment endures –
Revel in the present,
This moment is yours
To notice the stillness
And savour repose
With the warmth of the sun
And the scent of a rose.

– Emma Canning.

Matters Piscatorial

I '**VE** tried it from the riverbank,
I've tried it from the bridge,
I've tried the pond where bullrush grow
Just along the ridge;
I've tried out different kinds of reel
And changed the types of rod,
But they were not quite suitable,
It all seemed rather odd.
I've tested varied kinds of bait
And special brands of lore,
But the fish still swam round languidly,
Just like they did before.
I've even bought the waterproofs
So I could feel "in tune",
But oilskins and sou'westers
Don't look quite right in June.
I got myself an outdoor flask,
More robust than the old,
But, when I came to drink the tea,
Yes, you've guessed it – cold!
So I will admit defeat;
I'll neither sulk nor pout.
Now, in matters piscatorial,
Simply count me out!

– Brian H. Gent.

Child And Butterfly

DETERMINED look on curl-framed face,
Outstretched hands and feet that fly,
Dainty body full of grace
As child pursues swift butterfly!

First here, then there, from flower to flower,
Lightly twinkling butterfly lands,
Child lunges, clutches with all power
Then stares, amazed, at empty hands!

Child loves this game with butterfly –
Faster, faster, quicken the pace!
Butterfly, bored, soars off in the sky,
Child watches it go with small, sad face.

– Eileen Hay.

Arrival

I'M sitting here in the wee small hours,
I dare not go to sleep —
I'm waiting for those signs that herald
The patter of tiny feet.

We've had extra feeding and exercise,
The "is she, isn't she" games,
The endless lists of what to do
And the fun of choosing names.

The books have been read, the details planned,
So everything is prepared —
The shopping trips for the things to have in,
The trying not to feel scared.

The waiting is over, the process has started,
The hours of labour are here,
The anxious eyes that are fixed on mine
Take comfort from having me near.

A few years ago she was born in this room,
It's strange how the years have flown,
And my dearest companion, who's grown by my side,
Now has five bonnie pups of her own!

– Eliza Barret.

Little Tea Bag

HELLO, little tea bag!
I wonder where you've been?
Where is it you were lurking
Before you came upon the scene?
Perhaps it was Darjeeling,
Assam or Tibet,
Or in regions far away
We've not discovered yet.
Sometimes you are coloured green
Or taste of tropic fruits;
Whatever pleases palates,
You'll have one that suits.
You have come a long, long way
Since strainers, pots and spoons,
Where ladies in their boudoirs
Sipped tea in the afternoons.
Once you were so precious,
(And without doubt still are)
Though we don't lock you in a box
But keep you in a jar.
You are now the nation's choice
At dinner, lunch or suppers,
For life would be unthinkable
Without refreshing cuppas.

– *Brian H. Gent.*

The First Signs

THE first signs are here
That autumn is pending –
That new evening chill
Shows that summer is ending.

The crisp, hazy dawns
With the mist slowly clearing,
The days drawing in –
All signs autumn's nearing.

So stock up with logs
And with baskets of kindling.
We'll soon need our fires
Now that summer is dwindling!

– Eileen Hay.

Special Combination

MOTHER NATURE'S lit her candles
On the chestnut tree,
They sparkle in the noonday sun,
A lovely sight to see.
Those little flower clusters,
Pretty, fresh and new,
Greet the brand new morning
With their alabaster hue.
And when, at last, they ripen,
And turn to chocolate brown,
Their spiky shells will open
And start to tumble down.
But Nature has just one more trick
Well hidden up her sleeve,
Which every little schoolboy
Is most happy to perceive.
What better combination
Could make a young heart sing
Than a pocket full of conkers
And a little ball of string?

– Brian H. Gent.

The Hay Loft

UP the ladder, old and rusty,
Into air that's dim and dusty;
Autumn sunshine sweetly gleams
Through the gaps in ancient beams.

Flickering golden sunlight dapples
On the beetle-shiny apples
Stored in boxes lined with hay,
In the age-old country way.

Where the amber light is lancing
Lazy, hazy dustmotes dancing;
On the walls, on hand-made nails,
Pitchforks, scythes and milking pails.

In the rafters fat bees blundering,
Sated from their poppy plundering;
Sparrows darting in and out
For the grain that's strewn about.

All is silent, heavy, brooding,
And I feel that I'm intruding.
Still I'm loth to leave this balm –
Timeless peacefulness and calm.

– Eileen Hay.

Chestnuts And Bonfires

MY childhood memories of autumn are of a world filled with God's glory. In the years immediately following the war, going to village cricket matches was a real joy. For so long the skies had been filled with enemy aircraft, barrage balloons and exploding doodlebugs. Now above us there were floating clouds, a shining sun and swallows swooping in the air.

My father played for the team and we watched closely when he went in to bat. Would he score a duck or hit a memorable century?

There was an added bonus in the shape of a picnic. Wartime rationing was in full force, so it would be tomato and cucumber sandwiches, hard-boiled eggs that had been preserved in isinglass and a cake with the barest hint of sugar. A rug was spread in the long grass outside the boundary and we enjoyed the feast to the accompaniment of buzzing insects, over-enthusiastic wasps, fluttering butterflies and wild flowers.

When we tired of watching the game there were other pastimes close at hand. We searched the hedges for late birds' nests and sometimes came upon a thrush's or blackbird's hideaway with a batch of eggs inside. We never took them as that was against the rules.

Dandelion stems could be turned into small trumpets that emitted a loud blast of sound when blown through. There was a tree with low branches that presented a stiff challenge to the would-be climber, and just behind the cricket pavilion was a small pond. Sometimes you would see two frog eyes staring up at you from a floating bunch of leaves.

Hide and seek amongst the bushes was a favourite, as was searching for blackberries and eating them straight off the bushes. It was worth it even though we ended up covered in scratches and nettle stings.

They were wonderful, happy times lived out under the warm September sunshine, and when the game was over, we picked up our secondhand bicycles and wove our way home along the sunken lanes.

The poet Wordsworth captured this atmosphere when he looked back to his childhood.

"There was a time when meadow, grove and stream,
The earth, and every common sight

By the Rev. David Bryant.

To me did seem
    Apparelled in celestial light."
    In other words, children have a special awareness of the wonder of God's world which can easily be lost as we grow older. Perhaps this explains the passage in St Matthew's gospel.
    "At that time the disciples came to Jesus saying, 'Who is the greatest in the kingdom of heaven?' And calling to him a child he put him in the midst of them and said, 'Truly I say to you, unless you turn and become like children, you will never enter the kingdom of heaven'."

BONFIRES feature strongly in my memories of autumn. I can still recall that rich smell of smoke as weeds, dead flowers and leaves were piled in a corner of the garden and set alight. Sometimes they would smoulder for days.
    When the flames had died away and the embers glowed hot, we buried potatoes in the hot ash. An hour later we fished them out, charred and half-baked, and tucked into them. Another cooking method was to place a potato in an empty tin and throw it into the flames. The results were, to say the least, variable!
    An old favourite was the smoke game. You threw a thick layer of grass cuttings on to the flames, producing a dense blanket of smoke. The challenge was to run through it with closed eyes, holding your breath. The winner was the one who could do it the most times without getting a coughing fit. Running eyes and clothes that smelled of burning leaves for days was the inevitable outcome.
    Here was another pointer to God, for he is often described in terms of fire. Moses found his presence in a bush that spontaneously burst into flames in the noonday heat of the desert. In his often-sung hymn, Charles Wesley speaks of God as the fire of love.
    "O Thou who earnest from above,
    The pure celestial fire to impart,
    Kindle a flame of sacred love,
    On the mean altar of my heart."
    So those autumn bonfires were a reminder that the whole world is "charged with the glory of God."

CONKERS are a tradition of autumn. There was a tall horse chestnut tree in our garden growing close to a creosoted fence. One of the palings was missing, so you could lever yourself up on to the bottom branch. Then it was a matter of scrambling up through the foliage, filling your pockets with conkers as you climbed ever higher. Often the biggest specimens were at the end of branches and you had to crawl out listening to the creaking wood, hoping it would not snap off, plunging you to the ground!
    Down on terra firma, preparations began in earnest. The conkers were removed from their husks and put on top of the range to dry and harden. When they were

ready, a hole was pierced through the middle with a meat skewer. Those that survived without splitting were threaded on to string. The winner was the one who managed to split or crack his opponent's chestnut by whacking it.

When I look back I realise what an incredible miracle lies behind trees. Years ago, somebody must have planted a chestnut in the garden, and as the seasons and years went by it grew into a sapling, a young tree and then a giant, 40 feet high, producing leaves, twigs, branches, roots and a massive trunk. Each year it flowered and a new batch of chestnuts was born.

The prophet Isaiah pictured all this wonder in creation: "For you shall go out in joy, and be led forth in peace: the mountains and the hills before you shall break forth into singing, and all the trees of the field shall clap their hands."

The glory of autumn and the passing seasons is summed up for me in the words of Hildegard of Bingen, the 12th-century mystic and nun.

"The blowing wind,
The mild, moist air,
The exquisite greening
Of trees and grasses –
In their beginning,
In their ending,
They give God their praise." ∎

A Country Calendar For *Autumn*

"Give me juicy autumnal fruit, ripe and red from the orchard." – **Walt Whitman.**

"September is my favourite month, particularly in Cornwall. I felt, even as a child, that if you get a wonderful day in September, you think: 'This could be one of the last, the summer is nearly over.' If you get a wonderful day in May, you think: 'So what, there's more coming.'" – **Tim Rice.**

■ The full moon that lands closest to the autumn equinox is the Harvest Moon, so named because, before artificial lighting, farmers took advantage of the full moon's light to harvest their crops.

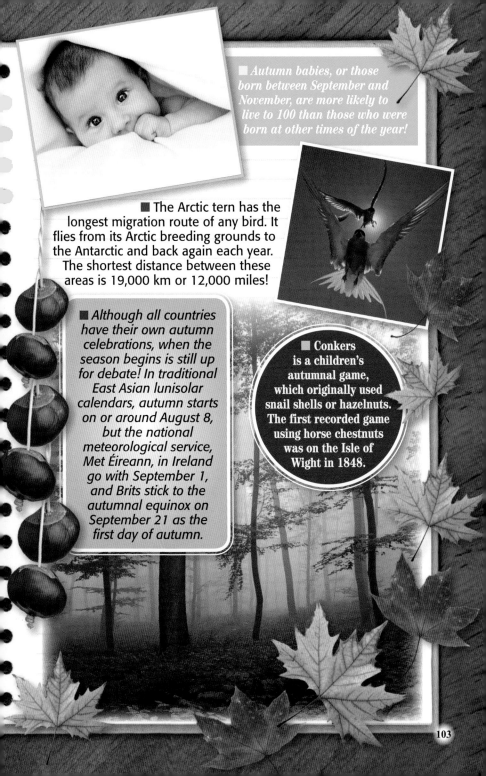

■ *Autumn babies, or those born between September and November, are more likely to live to 100 than those who were born at other times of the year!*

■ The Arctic tern has the longest migration route of any bird. It flies from its Arctic breeding grounds to the Antarctic and back again each year. The shortest distance between these areas is 19,000 km or 12,000 miles!

■ *Although all countries have their own autumn celebrations, when the season begins is still up for debate! In traditional East Asian lunisolar calendars, autumn starts on or around August 8, but the national meteorological service, Met Éireann, in Ireland go with September 1, and Brits stick to the autumnal equinox on September 21 as the first day of autumn.*

■ Conkers is a children's autumnal game, which originally used snail shells or hazelnuts. The first recorded game using horse chestnuts was on the Isle of Wight in 1848.

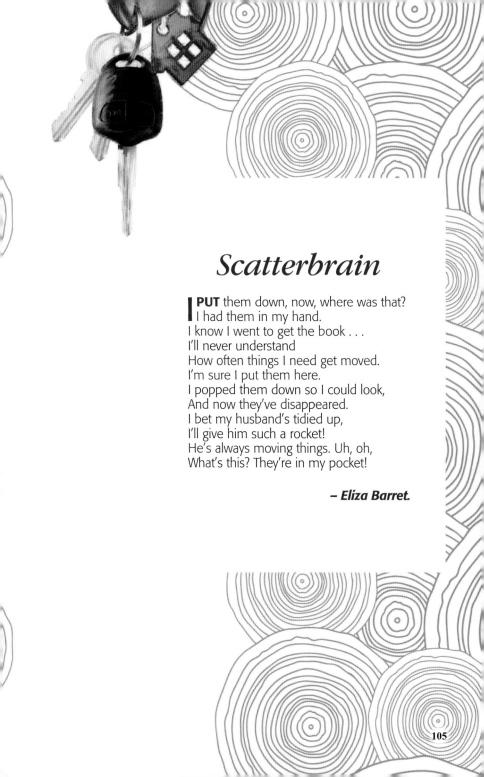

Scatterbrain

I PUT them down, now, where was that?
I had them in my hand.
I know I went to get the book . . .
I'll never understand
How often things I need get moved.
I'm sure I put them here.
I popped them down so I could look,
And now they've disappeared.
I bet my husband's tidied up,
I'll give him such a rocket!
He's always moving things. Uh, oh,
What's this? They're in my pocket!

– Eliza Barret.

Old Wives' Tales

I'LL happily walk under ladders,
Cracked mirrors don't cause me unease;
I don't think spilled salt is unlucky,
Or that troubles will turn up in threes.

I'll step on the cracks in the pavement,
I don't have my own lucky charm;
Indoors, I have opened umbrellas.
I don't think it's done any harm.

I've placed brand-new shoes on the table,
I'll get out of bed either side;
I didn't wear old, new and borrowed
And blue, for my turn as a bride.

No, I never pay much attention
To myths . . . although maybe I should?
I'll just have to hope it won't matter;
Keep my fingers crossed – and touch wood!

– Emma Canning.

The Charms Of Autumn

SUMMERTIME is ending,
The nights are drawing in.
The cooler days of autumn
Will shortly now begin.

The hedgerow harvest's ripening
And wild things eat their fill.
Their autumn feast enables them
To bear the winter chill.

And humans like to make the most
Of each bright autumn day
By walking in our lovely woods,
Through nature's fair display.

So, even when the nights are long,
There's beauty to be found
As autumn travels through our land
And spreads its charms around.

– Rosemary Bennett.

Love Letters

IT'S not so very long ago
That letters from a loving beau
Would make a young girl dance with joy,
Such *bon mots* from a smitten boy!

She'd read it blushingly and smile,
Then add it to the growing pile
Tied up in ribbons made of lace
And hidden in a secret place!

The e-mail lacks all such romance –
The girl will read it at a glance
And maybe think, well, that's quite sweet!
And then she'll simply press Delete!

And texting simply can't be right –
The effortless "c u tonite"
And "luv u babe" will not bring tears
Of joy throughout the coming years!

I wonder if the wheel will turn
And young men once again will learn
The magical, beguiling art
Of writing letters from the heart!

– Eileen Hay.

Old Favourites

WHAT shall I read? On my bookshelves I find
Novels and volumes of every kind:
Thrillers and romance, science and history,
Stories of fantasy, folklore and mystery.

Books from my youth – I'd be instantly sent
Back to my childhood, where long hours were spent
Caught up in tales of adventures galore.
If I choose these, I'll be spellbound once more.

The latest bestsellers – unopened, brand new –
Hours of intrigue to look forward to.
And yet, in the habit of many booklovers,
I so often reach for the old, tattered covers.

These are my favourites; all dog-eared and creased,
Read so many times – oh, a hundred, at least.
Yet still I'll select them and once again start
To leaf through each one, though I know them by heart.

To read them again is to happily spend
A cosy few hours with an old, faithful friend.
Contentment and tranquillity, guaranteed –
You're never alone when you've something to read.

– Emma Canning.

The Moonlit Hare

THE moon was full in the autumn sky
And silvered every field and hill;
The hare sat, head up, ears alert,
His graceful body statue-still.

I loved his timeless silhouette,
This beast of legend, magic, lore.
So large a part the hare has played
In fairy tales and tales of yore.

But then, nearby, the haunting cries
Of hunting owls had startled him,
And off he raced with flying bounds,
So elegant in line and limb.

I watched him disappear from sight,
His instincts deep within his blood;
I turned from moonlit, magic myth
And tramped home through the earthbound mud!

– Eileen Hay.

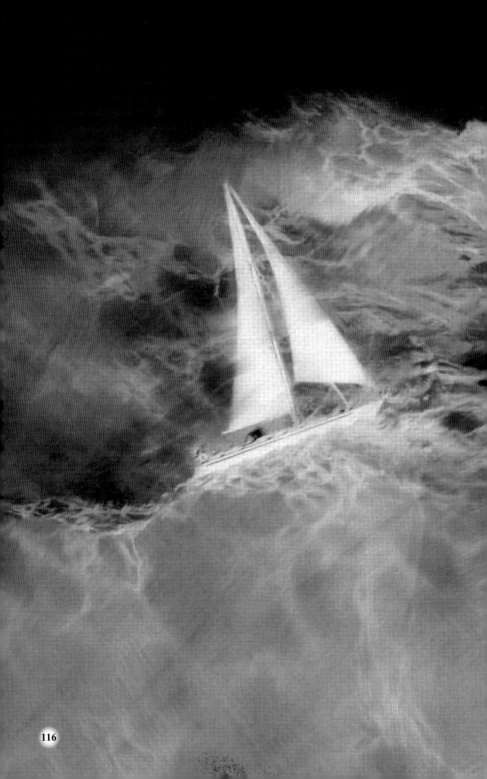

Song Of The Sea

H**ELP** me, Lord God, to sail my boat
Across life's restless sea;
Guide me and protect me, Lord,
Steer me safely home to Thee.

Remember me when tides run fast
And my boat is hard to steer;
Direct me to calm waters, Lord,
Safe in heaven's haven fair.

When storm clouds gather overhead,
And billows rage and roar,
Be with me in my hour of need –
Take me safely back to shore.

When I hear Thee call me home,
And my sailing days are past,
I will drop my anchor gladly
In heaven's harbour, safe at last.

– Edward Mitchell.

Our Daily Bread

AFTER wondering for a long time what we could do to celebrate the Harvest Festival, a group of people at our church decided to hold a vegetable show to display the many examples that we could find of God's bountiful provision. The signs of new life that were so obvious in the spring and had heralded the promise of good things to come had grown into a wonderful array of sights and smells that ensured we would be fed all winter through.

There is a large area of allotment plots next to the church and we felt that we should take advantage of the proximity of things being grown to provide tasty food and the pleasure of working in the open air.

Flowers, fruit and vegetables were there in abundance. The many classes that could be entered included the inevitable one for "biggest marrow" as well as numerous other classes of flowers and vegetables. We knew that the "oddest-shaped vegetable" would be popular, and that proved correct.

We were aware that these would never be of a standard to be displayed in the Chelsea Flower Show, or other

such national competitions, but these offerings were to show that things could be grown for the sheer enjoyment of it, and to bear witness to the wonders of God's creation all around us.

The children were not ignored, either. They had their own competitions – for example for the longest runner bean, as well as showing their skill in flower-arranging in jam-jars, and many other activities. They could take part in these while the adults were enjoying a well-deserved piece of cake and cup of tea.

The many displays of our handiwork helped us to exclaim with the psalmist, "Let all creation rejoice before the Lord".

However, we were very much aware that there had been many times in the history of this country when such a variety of food and its riotous colour was not possible. Unfortunately, this continues today in many parts of the world, where the abundance of God's provision is no longer evident and there is very little rejoicing over the harvest. ▶

Thinkstockphotos.

By Kathrine Davey, Mansfield Methodist preacher.

▶ That is sad, and we are truly thankful for those who go to those places in order to bring help to people in such need.

There are many countries that have too much, and we often do not share God's bounty with our neighbours, so they are left wanting. In other words, it is the fault of God's people, not of God, whose very nature is love.

A lot of such misfortunes are because the weather (and the opportunity for farming) is seasonal. While we in the west do not have a rainy season – although some might say that this continues throughout the year in Britain – much of our food has a variety that is dependent on the time of the year.

The enjoyment of various foods at different times of the year is now an experience lost because of the advent of supermarkets and availability of food all year round.

This seems a pity, because we are forgetting the proper time for each fruit and vegetable – for example, the wait for fresh strawberries which means that summer is on its way, or a warming stew made from seasonal vegetables to cheer us during those long winter nights.

GOD works in seasons, too, and He expects us to recognise the season, or right time, for food. In fact, we are told in the psalms that all the animals, both great and small, "look to you (that is, to God) to give them their food in the proper time".

The "proper time" will differ among the animals, or even among people, but we are assured that God knows when this "proper" time is, and that He meets our needs, at whatever time of the day or night.

I am sure that this is why in the Lord's Prayer we are told to ask for our "daily" bread. If God only gives us enough bread for today, then it means we have to ask again tomorrow, ensuring our dependence on God to provide for our needs.

I believe Jesus uses the word "bread" because it tells us not to ask for "cake". That is to say, he only promises to meet our needs, not provide us with life's little luxuries.

If we feel that we have more than the bare necessities of life, then this indeed is an added blessing from the Lord, and we should be grateful that we have such abundance.

Jesus's teaching on prayer reminds me very much of the story of the children of Israel and their wanderings in the desert, when God gave them their daily ration of manna, shown in the painting opposite. The people had to learn the hard way that God would provide only enough food for each day's needs.

What they discovered was that, if they gathered too much, trying to hoard some for the next day, they soon found that it had gone past its sell-by date and turned mouldy!

The vegetable show at our church concluded with a joyful time of songs of praise. We raised our voices to the God and Father of us all, who spared no

expense in showing His care for us, both in the world around and ultimately in the giving of His son.

This was echoed in the care given by so many of the congregation to the fruits of garden and allotment, which they had come together to celebrate.

And we all came to realise that we can care only because He first cared for us. ■

A Country Calendar For *Autumn*

"No spring nor summer beauty hath such grace as I have seen in one autumnal face." – John Donne.

■ Monarch butterflies begin their gruelling migration south around this time of year. Their 2500-mile voyage takes them from the Great Lakes in Canada to the warm Central Mexican fir forests where they spend the winter – and have a well-deserved rest!

■ *A haar is a coastal fog that occurs typically in the autumn along lands bordering the North Sea. It is a phrase used mainly in eastern Scotland. Variations on the word include har, hare, harl, harr and hoar and it is thought that the origin may be Saxon.*

"Fall has always been my favourite season. The time when everything bursts with its last beauty, as if nature had been saving up all year for the grand finale." – Lauren DeStefano.

■ Most popular in the north of Britain, bonfire toffee was usually a home-made confectionery made from black treacle. It's not really clear why the sweet became associated with Guy Fawkes Night, but it was also known as treacle toffee, cinder toffee, Plot toffee, Tom Trot, claggum (in Scotland) and loshin du (in Wales).

■ *Lavender bushes can be pruned in autumn ready for winter. Essential oil of lavender has antiseptic and anti-inflammatory properties and was used in hospitals during World War I to disinfect floors and walls.*

■ *The Ancient Greeks had an interesting theory about autumn. They believed Persephone had to spend a third of the year in the underworld with her husband, Hades, while her mother, Demeter, the Greek goddess of grain and harvest, was so heartbroken that she allowed the crops on Earth to die until her daughter returned to her in the spring.*

On The Cards

I BOUGHT myself a floral box
To keep my cards within;
Occasion cards of every kind;
It's full right to the brim.
Get-well cards and christenings,
Just moved house, congratulations,
New baby with its joyous news,
"Well done" write the relations.
Then there's aunties, uncles, cousins,
Grandparents, nephews and nieces,
The cat and dog and goldfish,
Mum and Dad, "Love you to pieces".
If it's on the cards I'll have it –
Christmas lights and bulging socks;
Country views and cartoon humour,
All inside my floral box.

– Dorothy McGregor.

Happy Birthday

Merry Christmas

HAPPY BIRTHDAY

Happy Birthday

HAPPY FATHER'S DAY

Sealed With A Loving Kiss

PUTTING pen to paper
Has become a dying art.
A letter that's handwritten
No longer plays a part.

An e-mail's so much quicker,
But how can it compare
With words that someone's chosen
And penned with loving care?

Yes, speed is of the essence
In this crazy world today.
Technology rules over all,
Computers are "the way".

But handwriting is personal
And is unique to you.
With every line and dot and curve
Your character shines through.

Putting words on paper,
In a script that's yours alone,
Can never, ever be replaced
By texting on a phone.

So send to me a letter
On paper, by a pen.
A letter I can hold and read
And keep and hold again.

A truly personal letter,
That's what I really miss,
With writing on the envelope –
SWALK (Sealed With A Loving Kiss).

– Greta Ward.

Dreams

THERE are some dreams which never die,
So keep them fresh and new,
And, if the world should turn away,
To thine own self be true.

Some wishes take a long, long time;
Keep wishing just the same.
Don't give up and don't despair.
This life's a waiting game.

Some hopes are like a ray of light,
A rainbow after rain,
And one day soon you're sure to find
Your dreams were not in vain.

– Iris Hesselden.

The Right Approach

IT'S autumn, the trees are a beautiful sight,
Their glorious colours fill me with delight.
Plump blackberries beckon, ripe apples abound,
They're ready to pick or they'll fall to the ground.

Soon cosy fires welcome us as it gets dark,
We take healthy walks by the sea, in the park.
We're making the most of dry days not too cold,
Enjoying late sunshine as summer's grown old.

There's so much to treasure as leaves flutter by,
As squirrels get busy and greedy gulls cry,
The cheeks of the children are rosy and glowing;
They can't wait for winter and days when it's snowing.

Then, when it arrives, there'll be pleasures galore,
With hot tasty stews, happy evenings in store.
Bad weather we'll combat, then snuggle inside.
Prepare for the worst, then take it in our stride.

We'll relish the fireside, radio and TV,
Our reading and music such great company.
Dear friends and relations and good conversation,
For laughter and hobbies are winter's salvation.

A meal out, a theatre, a shopping day's treat,
A chat and a laugh with the folk that we meet.
Then, in the mid-winter, to bring us good cheer
Christmas magic, then after, a hope-filled New Year.

– Chrissy Greenslade.

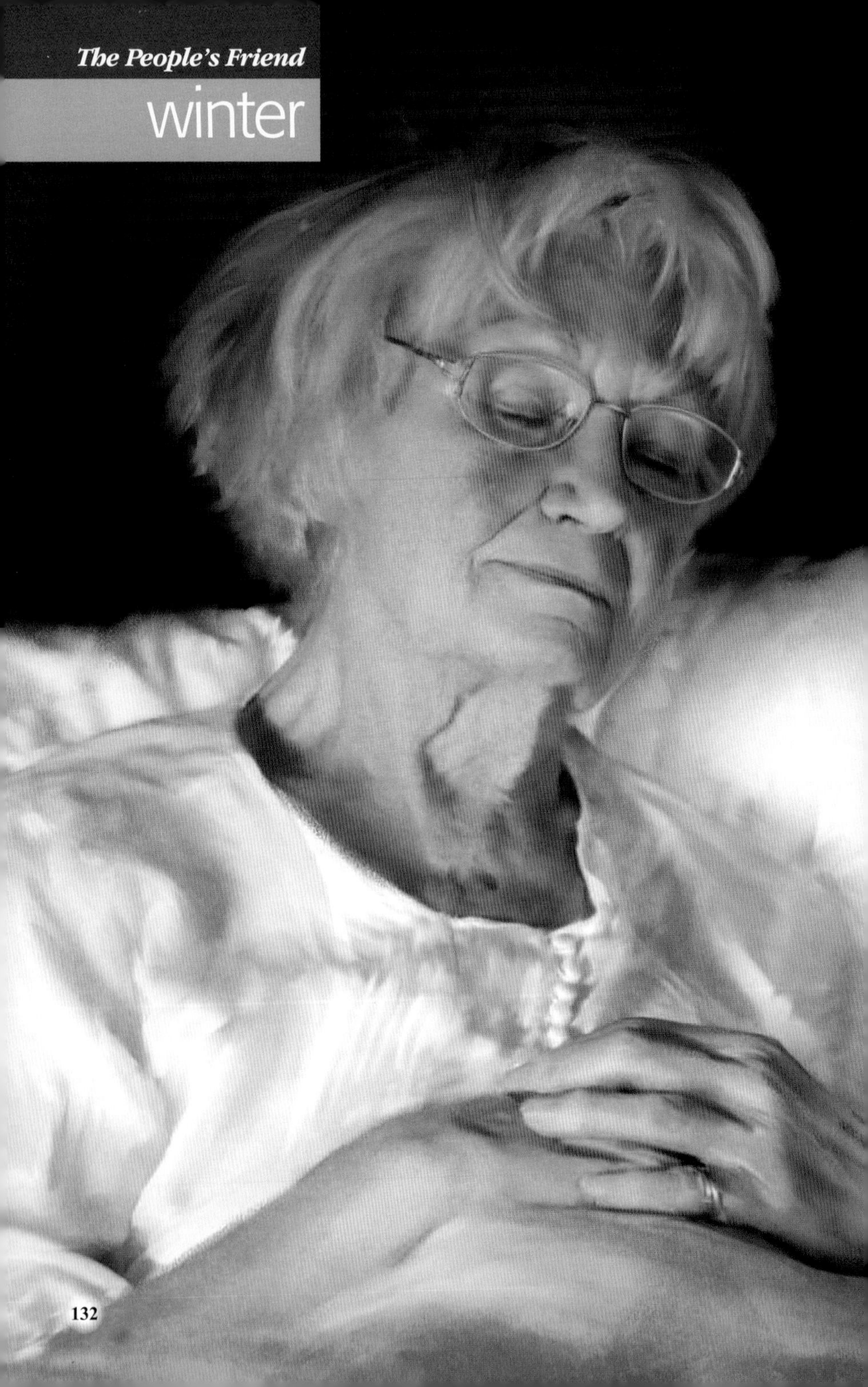

Sleep Tight

I'VE had a nasty cold and it's been keeping me awake,
So I've compiled a list of helpful measures I can take!
Before I go to bed this evening, here's what I shall do:
A nice relaxing bubble bath; a gentle stretch or two.
I'll organise tomorrow's tasks, that way I'll clear my head,
Then make some herbal tea and find a book to read in bed.
I'll turn off my alarm clock, wear my cosiest nightgown,
Use my scented eye-pillow to help me settle down.
I'll keep my throat sweets handy lest I wake up with a cough . . .
But I did none of these things, 'cause I must have nodded off!

– Emma Canning.

Winds Of Change

WITH gusto they all twirl around,
Silently, without a sound,
High up in their lofty towers,
In sunshine or in sudden showers,
Happily to work away,
With ne'er a thought of take-home pay.
No need for FTSE or Dow Jones,
Bulls and Bears or mobile phones,
And if we are prepared to wait,
We'll have cheap warmth for winter's grate.
A pleasant change from food that's tinned,
Now farms are harvesting the wind!

– Brian H. Gent.

Moonlight

THE earth is bathed in moonlight.
Its soft and silver sheen
On forest, field and mountainside
Transforms the country scene.

On cottages and castles
The silver moonbeams play,
And add a touch of magic
To the world we know by day.

On frosty nights in wintertime,
Earth sparkles 'neath the moon,
And summer nights of pure delight
Seem almost bright as noon.

The lovely, silver moonlight
Transforms the world we know
Into a new, enchanting place,
Bathed in its gentle glow.

– Rosemary Bennett.

Rain

WET-PEWTER pavements,
Grey misty shrouds
Draping every treetop
Under lowering clouds.
Dull gleam of puddles,
Lamps on by day,
Colour leached from landscapes,
Daylight kept at bay.
Raincoated people
Bowed in the storm,
Longing for the moment
They'll be home and warm!

– Eileen Hay.

Seasons Come, Seasons Go

TODAY was the first day I felt really cold. A chilly gust of wind caught me off guard on the way to my local shop for the newspaper, making me wish I'd worn a coat. Much as I love the garden and the outdoors, it actually felt good to get back indoors and put the kettle on!

Suddenly I became aware that most of the summer's blossom is now past and the trees are heavy with leaves that are starting to discolour, droop and fall. The squirrels in our local park sense the changes and are busy gathering their hibernation store. The birds are preparing for their long journey to warmer climes.

"All is safely gathered in,
'Ere the winter storms begin."

There's no avoiding it. It's that time of year again – time to prepare for winter. Time to get the heavier duvet out of the hot press, check there's plenty of heating oil in the tank and perhaps make an appointment to see the doctor for a 'flu jab.

Each year we are given advice on keeping "warm and well" during the cold season, everything from tips on insulation to simple encouragement to be good neighbours, not too shy to check others are OK. When the Met Office issues a warning of an imminent "cold snap" we need to ensure we have extra food in the freezer and that any medication is well stocked up, so we don't have to make unnecessary journeys out into the cold.

Looking back, 2010 brought a particularly severe winter to our part of the world, with record low temperatures. I can remember it was physically painful to be outside, the cold penetrating however many layers I had wrapped up in! So apart from the opportunity for a snowball fight and building a snowman, we stayed inside as much as possible.

There seems to be a higher incidence of depressive illness during these months, and researchers have linked it to the shorter days and long, dark nights. The amount of sunlight affects the levels of the hormone melatonin in the human body, changing sleep patterns and causing lethargy and despondency. It's even been given an appropriate name – Seasonal Affective Disorder or SAD! It just confirms what we've known all along – bright, sunny days make us feel happier.

▶

Thinkstockphotos.

By the Rev. Andrew Watson.

▶ Nature's seasons give us a pattern of life we are wise to note – that sometimes things "get worse before they get better", that there will be dark days and challenging times, but then things will brighten again, giving occasion for fresh gladness! As the chorus in the musical "Les Miserables" sing in the finale:

"For the wretched of the Earth there is a flame that never dies,
Even the darkest night will end and the sun will rise."

A S I write this, the news has been full of harrowing reports of how Christians and other minorities are being cruelly oppressed in various countries around the world. It's nothing new. Jesus warned his disciples they would be hated because of him, and numerous references in the New Testament, including the last book, Revelation, encourage believers to keep the faith as a "winter" of difficulty sets in.

Even if we do not experience actual physical persecution for our beliefs, we all share common hardships such as sickness, separation, unemployment and so on. Yes, there will be "winter", but our Lord has experienced human suffering first hand with us and for us, so that we can trust in his promise of an eternal "spring". And each year God gives a reminder of our blessed future in Nature as the snowdrops and crocuses poke their way up defiantly through the frost!

The Old Testament prophet, Isaiah, had to predict tragic news, that Jerusalem would be conquered like a tree being felled. But he didn't end there. In Chapter 11 he was given to foresee that from the seemingly dead stump a fruitful "branch" would sprout. This person would bring powerfully an end to evil, rescue the poor and downtrodden, and people from all nations would eventually unite to live together in heavenly peace.

"The wolf will live with the lamb, the leopard will lie down with the goat, the calf and the lion and the yearling together, and a little child will lead them." (Isaiah 11: 6)

Christ has already come and begun this profound work of renewal in people's hearts worldwide. As the Apostles' Creed states, "He will come again to judge the living and the dead."

In Matthew 25 Jesus tells three parables which are effectively instructions on how people should prepare for his return, and the "winter" we may face before then.

"The Ten Bridesmaids" teaches us always to be full of the Holy Spirit so we can witness effectively for him, like those carrying bright lamps to welcome and light the way for the arriving "Bridegroom". The parable of the "Talents" teaches us to invest whatever gifts and resources we've been given to advance the kingdom of the returning King. "The Sheep and Goats" teaches us to show care and compassion to all in need, for this identifies genuine followers of the Good Shepherd.

As we brace ourselves for another winter closing in, it's only wise to make

preparations, holding on to our hope that, in due course, the cold and dark will pass and spring will return.

The long night will end. The sun will rise. Our spirits will lift once more in the warmth of Christ's new day. ▮

A Country Calendar For *Winter*

"Winter is the time for comfort, for the touch of a friendly hand and for a talk beside the fire: it is the time for home."
– Edith Sitwell.

"Look round and round upon this bare bleak plain, and see even here, upon a winter's day, how beautiful the shadows are! Alas! It is the nature of their kind to be so. The loveliest things in life, Tom, are but shadows; and they come and go, and change and fade away, as rapidly as these!"
– Charles Dickens.

■ A sprig of holly has long been a symbol of Christmas, but it has other associations in folklore, too. Holly was believed to frighten off witches and protect the home from thunder and lightning. Putting a sprig of holly on the bedpost was thought to bring sweet dreams, making a tonic from holly would cure a cough, and arguments were always best settled under a holly tree!

■ According to legend, we will have a cold winter if squirrels build their nests low in trees and gather nuts early.

■ **The record for the most people making snow angels simultaneously on the same site is 8,962 at the State Capitol Grounds in Bismarck, North Dakota in 2007. What a sight that must have been!**

■ *In the 2014 Winter Olympics, the speed-skating team from the Netherlands won 23 medals in total – eight gold, seven silver and eight bronze. This meant that on their own, the Dutch speed-skating team would have finished sixth on the final countries' medal count!*

■ The low temperatures in winter can do strange things to precipitation! Hailstones are raindrops which have frozen on their way to the ground; snow is formed when water vapour in clouds freezes before it can turn into rain; sleet is primarily snow that has melted while falling; and freezing rain is formed when raindrops make it to earth before freezing on a cold surface such as roads or pavements.

Hiding Places

WHERE does all the wildlife go
To shelter from the wind and snow,
Small, scurrying voles and shrews and mice,
When all their world has frost and ice?

In their burrows, hide and nest
They snuggle close for warmth and rest;
In thick hedgerows and under leaves,
They hide and sleep away the freeze.

Squirrels' hoards can often bring,
On sunny days, imagined spring,
So out they scamper, find their store,
Then back to sleep till they want more.

But, oh, how welcome when birds find
Titbits and nuts and bacon rind,
Suet and seeds that I leave there
On my bird table to show I care!

– Chrissy Greenslade.

A Frosty Morning

THE hoar on the meadow lies crisp and white
As I walk with my thoughts at very first light.
The crunch of the grass 'neath my feet as I tread
Is the sole sound I hear save some birds overhead.
The air that I breathe is so cold and clear
It sharpens my mind to my God ever near.
My prayers offered up are earnest and bold
For nearest and dearest, for friends new and old.
My fingers and toes are frozen right through,
But my heart is so warm with fond thoughts of you!

– *George Hughes.*

Grow Your Own

EACH day of this new year ahead,
Holds challenges unknown.
The way we face them brings results
Of all the seeds we've sown.

Every seed of hope we plant
Will grow and remove fear,
For, when acceptance plays its part,
Courage and peace are here.

Then all the efforts that we make,
To smile more, not complain,
Will spread the sunshine that we need,
So calm and strength remain.

Filled with love and faith and joy,
With all the seeds we've sown
We'll find the garden of our heart
And soul has fully grown.

– Chrissy Greenslade.

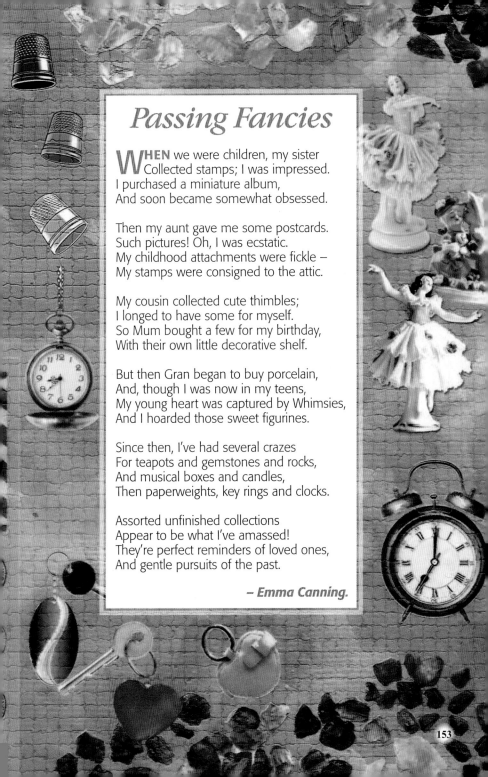

Passing Fancies

WHEN we were children, my sister
Collected stamps; I was impressed.
I purchased a miniature album,
And soon became somewhat obsessed.

Then my aunt gave me some postcards.
Such pictures! Oh, I was ecstatic.
My childhood attachments were fickle –
My stamps were consigned to the attic.

My cousin collected cute thimbles;
I longed to have some for myself.
So Mum bought a few for my birthday,
With their own little decorative shelf.

But then Gran began to buy porcelain,
And, though I was now in my teens,
My young heart was captured by Whimsies,
And I hoarded those sweet figurines.

Since then, I've had several crazes
For teapots and gemstones and rocks,
And musical boxes and candles,
Then paperweights, key rings and clocks.

Assorted unfinished collections
Appear to be what I've amassed!
They're perfect reminders of loved ones,
And gentle pursuits of the past.

– Emma Canning.

Little Bulbs

IN they go!
Those little friends,
Who'll cheer us through the snow.

All bedded in,
The right way up,
To help them thrive and grow.

Their shoots and leaves
Will soon appear
With every autumn shower.

And we'll be blessed
With nature's joy
Of every pretty flower.

– Nicola Herington.

Pamper Night

THIS evening I shall treat myself – a hot soak in the tub.
I'll have a pamper session with my brand-new body scrub.
I've many special toiletries in dainty little packs;
I'm certain to find something that will help me to relax!

Here's a set my friend gave me. Delightfully presented,
It's in a little basket: elegant and honey scented.
This mango set looks lovely, but I'm slightly apprehensive –
It's tied with silken ribbons and I fear it was expensive!

Perhaps I'll try the little almond gift box from my daughter,
With fragrant, pearly bubble bath to pour into the water.
Or shall I use the oils my grandson bought for me last year?
And should I light a candle to complete the atmosphere?

Oils, soaps and scrubs and creams – how do I pick the right one?
My candles are so pretty that it seems a shame to light one!
So many different products. Goodness, which one should I choose?
Oh, where's my shower gel? These sets look much too nice to use!

– Emma Canning.

Bells Of Gladness

RING out the Christmas bells, to send
Their messages of hope, to blend
With choirs, whose voices soar, to raise
Those carols filled with joy and praise.
Ring out the season's cheer, to bring
A warmth of thought in everything,
To spread around the world, to say,
"Goodwill in hearts for ever stay!"

– *Elizabeth Gozney.*

Changed Days

CHRISTMAS was very different for me last year; for the first time in 55 years I wasn't going home. That's because my father passed away at the beginning of the year and the family home has been sold.

As a single woman, no matter where I've lived, I've always returned to the family home for Christmas. I've been fortunate enough that all the parishes I've served in have been close enough to home, so that after the Christmas services I've been able to spend Christmas with my family. Not one has been missed over the years. Even after my mother died at the beginning of December nearly 20 years ago, my father and I still determined to put up the tree, have Christmas dinner and open presents.

Christmas is filled with so many good memories. Like all families we had our traditions, one of which was always having a real Christmas tree (one year it reached to the ceiling). My father was born in the Ukraine, the youngest of four children, and it was his task to chop down a tree every Christmas. Often we'd tie red apples to the lower branches, which is what

he used to do when he was a boy. I loved to lie under the tree and gaze up through the dense branches or to look into the glass baubles and see the room reflected in them.

Christmas was about living in a magical place with endless time to play, a time locked away from the world with sweets and chocolate on tap and figs, nuts and tangerines to eat, things we never ate any other time of year. I can remember the year my brother and I were given spacehoppers and spent hours pretending they were horses, negotiating a showjumping course we'd set up in the hallway with cushions and boxes.

On one occasion my mother cooked the turkey overnight and I went to sleep with the wonderful aroma wafting its way up the stairs. Then there was the time it snowed and my brother and I used an old roasting tin to sled down the garden path.

Every time I went home, no matter my age, it was a chance to pay homage to all those wonderful memories. So what did I do last year? I cherished the memories

By the Rev. Susan Sarapuk.

▶ and spent Christmas with friends. In fact, I quite enjoyed the opportunity to do something different.

It's a timely reminder that, much as we want things to stay the same for ever, life is about change. Yet we need roots, something that can always be relied upon.

In a challenging world, God is the unchanging factor – our foundation, our roots, our touchstone, like going home for Christmas and finding warmth and security and a place to rest and remember. We might go away, but when we return we breathe a sigh of recognition.

In the Old Testament, the Israelites were always encouraged to remember. Remember where you once were, remember how God delivered you out of adversity time and time again, remember how good He has been, remember the times of milk and honey.

But they were told to be prepared to move on, too. That might have been one of the failings of the Scribes and Pharisees, who wanted things to remain as they were because, even under Roman occupation, they still held religious power.

But change was coming. God was at work in Jesus, but they couldn't see it and in the end they were left behind.

Mary and Joseph were ready to go with God, even though they had no idea where He would lead them. All the things that had been their security were taken away from them as they fled to Egypt. They had no idea when they left Nazareth that they wouldn't be back for a while. So, when everything was changing around them, what could they depend on? God was their rock, the one unchanging power in their lives. He is the one unchanging power in our lives, too, even though we don't always recognise that.

WHEN I was growing up my parents didn't go to church, although they sent me and my brother to Sunday school. I knew all about the Nativity, and even though we didn't go to church at Christmas, I knew God was a part of it.

One of the great joys when I made a real commitment to Christ as a student was to go to church at Christmas and finally understand what it was all about. Eyes opened, heart engaged, it felt wonderful. Yet all those years of ignorance were wonderful, too, because of the warmth of family and home and, underlying it all, the belief that there was a God and He was looking after us.

Nothing is constant in our lives. Even families change. Technology and society are moving on so fast that I was left behind a long time ago, and I've turned into a grumpy old woman remembering the good old days.

Maybe we don't want our churches to change because we want a place of safety in a crazy world? But God has never allowed His people to stay in one place. He's always calling us to move on because He wants to call others into the Kingdom and we are the people He uses to do that.

So I know that, wherever I spend Christmas in following years, it will be good. I'll be thankful for the years of memories, thankful for parents who gave their

best to both me and my brother, thankful for the house in which I grew up, even though it now belongs to someone else. I'll start building some new memories, secure in the knowledge that God is with me and no matter the change in my circumstances, He is my rock. ▨

A Country Calendar For *Winter*

"O, wind, if winter comes, can spring be far behind?"
– Percy Bysshe Shelley.

■ The brightly coloured chaffinch is one of many birds that don a duller coat in winter to better blend in with the bare trees.

■ "Good Queen Charlotte", the German wife of George III, set up the first-known Christmas tree in Britain at Queen's Lodge, Windsor, in December, 1800, but it didn't become popular until the reign of Queen Victoria, when many of our Christmas traditions were established.

■ From January 22 to March 17, 1947, snow fell somewhere in the UK every single day. Several of these snowfalls were of 23.6 in (60 cm) or more. The level of snow in Upper Teesdale and the Denbighshire Hills reached an incredible 59.1 in (1.5 m). The weather was so severe that the Army had to be brought in to drop supplies to people trapped in their homes due to blocked roads and railways.

Thinkstockphotos.

■ The 15th-century Father Christmas was a figure that encouraged feasts and merry-making to celebrate Christ's birth. It wasn't until the Victorian era that he adopted the traditions of Santa Claus and started bringing presents to children, too.

■ In mediaeval times, traditional Christmas fare included roast swan, pheasants and peacocks – not turkey. A special treat was a roast boar's head decorated with holly and fruit.

"Surely everyone is aware of the divine pleasures which attend a wintry fireside; candles at four o'clock, warm hearth rugs, tea, a fair tea-maker, shutters closed, curtains flowing in ample draperies to the floor, whilst the wind and rain are raging audibly without."

– Thomas de Quincey.

Letters

MY little girl can almost read;
She's trying so hard to succeed.
It didn't take her long to get
The rhythm of the alphabet,
And very soon, in leaps and bounds,
She picked up the phonetic sounds.
She's thrilled that she's remembered how
The C - O - W spells "cow".
Her writing, too, is doing fine
(Though seldom staying on the line).

My little girl is older now;
She's suddenly grown up somehow;
She writes for pleasure every day
And books are never far away.
She's finished school and, truth to tell,
Those early lessons served her well.
With all examinations passed
She's ready for the world, at last;
Embarking on her new career,
Her chosen path is very clear.

My little girl's now married and
She lives in a far distant land.
And now that I am old and grey,
And those I've known have passed away,
My little girl, across the sea,
Still lifts her pen and writes to me.
Her letters travel many miles,
And bring a picture of her smiles
When she was small, but, oh, so bright,
And learning how to read and write.

– D.W. Turner.

167

Our
Favourite Bird

W^E British people love our birds,
That no-one can deny.
We love to listen to them sing
And watch them as they fly.

We give them tasty things to eat,
We like to see them thrive,
And, when the weather's really cold,
It helps them to survive.

But which bird is our favourite?
Although it's hard to choose
There is a bright and cheeky one
We'd really hate to lose.

It's friendly and appealing,
And cute and lively, too.
Its name is Robin Redbreast,
And it's loved the country through.

– Rosemary Bennett.

Hand In Hand

THE years have been kind as we've travelled through life,
You and I, side by side, hand in hand.
A lifetime has passed since the day that we wed
Yet together, steadfast, we still stand.

We met long ago and we kindled a love
That proved strong, and as deep as the ocean,
Unaware that our youthful and tender romance
Would bloom into a life-long devotion.

We gave to each other great comfort and strength
During days that were painful or troubled.
My memories, though, are of joyful events
When, through sharing, our triumphs were doubled.

With years of discovery, laughter and trust
Came secure, everlasting affection.
You've only to smile and our thoughts are in tune:
We've a sure and unfailing connection.

Yet still you delight and amuse me, my love;
You enrich every day of my life.
You captured my heart and for ever it's yours –
I'm so happy we're husband and wife.

– Emma Canning.

Winter Scene

SNOW-CRUSTED pavements, bitter cold,
Pale daylight fades in sunset gold.
Icy gales, the year is old,
This our winter scene.

Dreaming moon, star-silvered night,
Frost diamonds sparkling in the light.
Ghostly owls in whispering flight
In our winter scene.

Misted woodlands in the dawn,
Summer gladness long since gone.
Robins shiver on the lawn
In our winter scene.

Soon will Christmas lights appear,
Telling us of Christian cheer,
Bringing love instead of fear
In our winter scene.

Spare a thought for those in need,
Hungry people we must feed.
Think more of giving, less of greed
In our winter scene.

– Edward Mitchell.